JOIN US FOR A FUN WEEKEND!

© 2023-2024 CHELSEA KONG

ALL RIGHTS RESERVED. ALL IMAGES USED IN THIS BOOK ARE LICENSED COPIES FROM THEIR RESPECTFUL OWNERS INCLUDING FREEPIK, GHETTY IMAGES, CANVA, OTHERS. THIS BOOK OR ANY PORTION THEREOF MAY NOT BE REPRODUCED OR USED IN ANY MANNER WHATSOEVER WITHOUT THE EXPRESS WRITTEN PERMISSION OF THE PUBLISHER EXCEPT FOR THE USE OF BRIEF QUOTATIONS IN A BOOK REVIEW.

PRINTED IN 2023-2024, MADE IN TORONTO, CANADA
ISBN: 978-1-998335-04-6
LIBRARY AND ARCHIVES CANADA

Worship

It is to honor or show deep respect for super being or supernatural power.

It is to give great or extravagant respect, honor, or devotion.

Focus on the Lord.
Dance for the Lord.

Read the Bible every day.
The Word of God is powerful.

Show God how much you love Him!

Put God first in everything you do.
Give God your full heart, soul, and mind.

Talk and pray with others about Jesus.
Remember what He has done.

Worship God in spirit and in truth.
Trust God in everything.

God wants us to become like Jesus.
Think, talk, and do what Jesus does.

Learn to say no to disobeying your parents and teachers and pray for them.

God is holy and wants respect.
Jesus loves us, but He is your King.

JOY

You will have joy.
It is great joy.

You will see right.
You will see the way God does.

You will be safe.
He hides you from the enemy.

You will have wisdom.
God's wisdom is great.

Church will be exciting.
Your prayers will be great.

Favour will come.
People will give things to you.

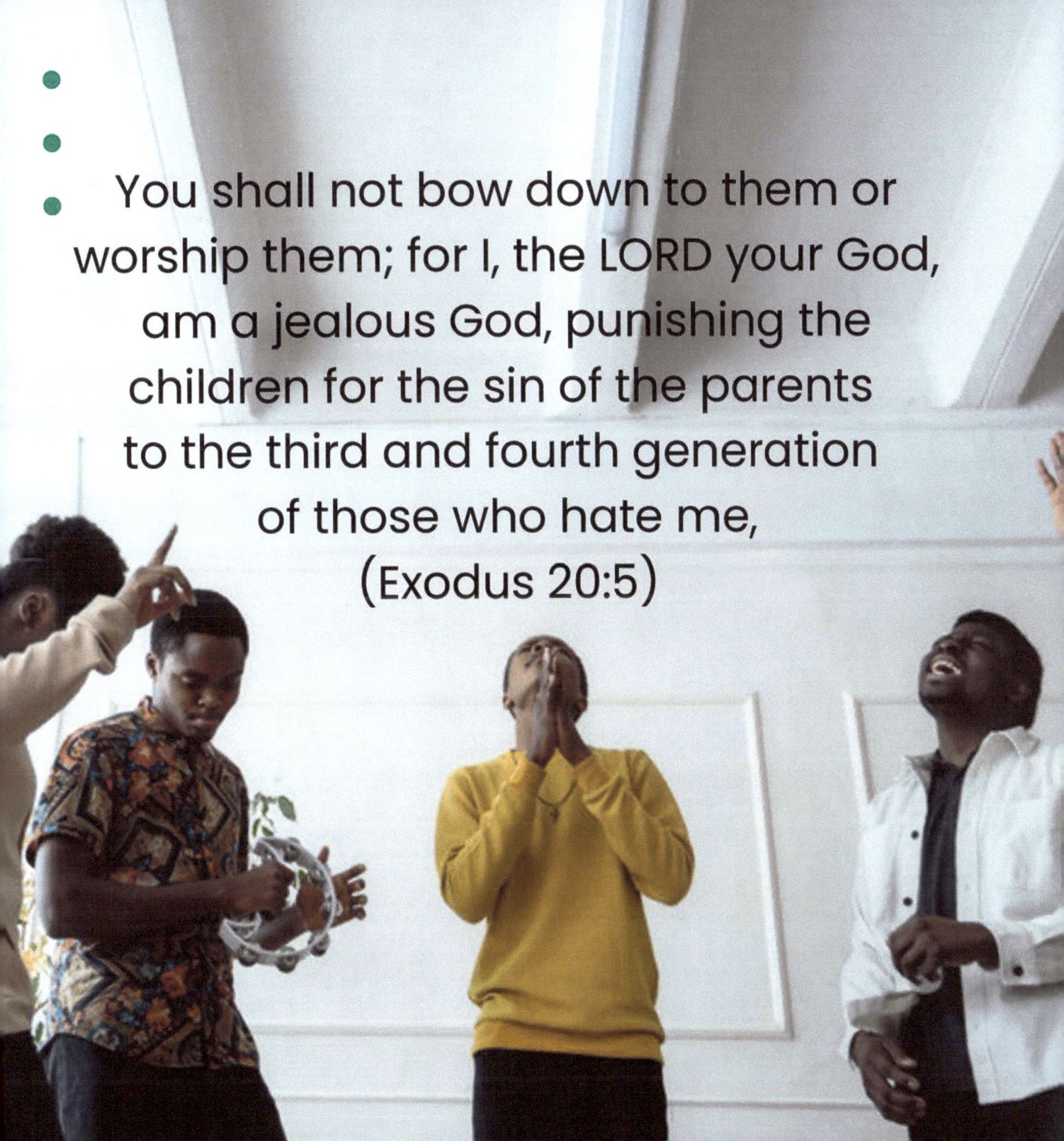

God wants us to obey Him all the time.
Go where Jesus tells you to do.

Remember that Jesus is coming back to earth as King and Judge.

SALVATION PRAYER

God, I know I sinned against you. Forgive me for the wrong that I have done. I believe that Jesus Christ died on the cross for me. That He rose from the grave so that after three days. I can have His long-lasting life. Come into my heart to be my Lord and Savior. I choose to turn away from my sins and I choose to follow you. Lead me to walk with you. Keep me safe and teach me your ways. Stop every bad thing in my life that has an open door to hurt me. Close those doors. Holy Spirit, fill me now in Jesus' name. Amen.

BAPTISM IN THE HOLY SPIRIT

Jesus, you are the one that fills me with Your Spirit. Come Holy Spirit and come into my life and fill me to overflow with Your presence. Come with your fire too. Thank you for the gift of tongues in Jesus' name. Amen.

Open your mouth and let the words come out that God gives you. It will be words that you don't know what they mean. You can ask God what it means. You need to let Him talk through you every day to grow this gift.

He will bring you closer to God and you will know Jesus more. You will have power from God to do great things and know things.

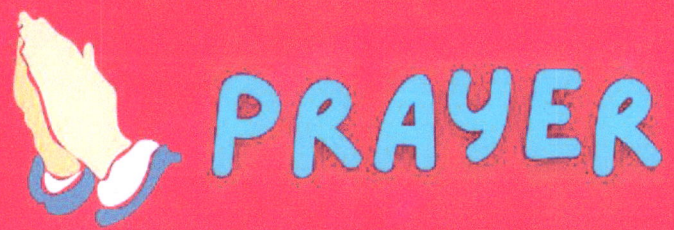

PRAYER

Thank you, Father, for this book on worship. Help me worship you like Jesus did. Holy Spirit, teach me how to worship God. I want to honour and love God with my whole heart. I give you my mind and soul too, in Jesus' name. Give me love and wisdom to help others. Give me a healthy fear of you to obey you all the time in Jesus' name. Amen.

MESSAGE FROM THE AUTHOR

Thank you for reading this book. I hope you can leave a good review to encourage me to write more books to teach children and adults. Worship the Lord all the time. He will give you honour too. Remember you can worship God anywhere you go. He wants us to love Him more than anything in this world. Then we will have the best things from God. He will not give us everything that we want. He knows what we will love.

OTHER PRODUCTS

- Knowing God
- How to Hear God's Voice
- New Life in Jesus
- Loving Israel
- God's Gifts/Spiritual Talents
- Meeting God
- Word Power
- Fruit of the Spirit
- The Tabernacle
- Bride for Jesus
- A Life of Prayer
- Live Free
- Who am I in Jesus
- Walk in Love
- God's Favor
- Man of God
- Woman of God
- How to Use Money
- God's Wisdom
- Fasting
- See Jerusalem and Bethany
- First Fruit Offering
- Feast of Trumpets
- Day of Atonement
- Feast of Tabernacles
- Counting the Omer
- Festival of Lights
- Glory, Presence, and Holy Spirit
- Live in God's Presence
- Pentecost
- See Galilee, Nazareth, and Tiberias
- Hear God Speak
- Knowing Jesus
- Knowing Holy Spirit
- A Healthy Life and Healthy Life Work Book
- Smokey the Cat
- Passover Unleavened Bread
- Resurrection Life
- The Blessing
- Revival
- Chelsea Learns Hebrew
- Thanksgiving
- Give Thanks
- Jesus Birth
- Loving Jesus: Bride and Groom
- Proverbs 31 Woman

OTHER PRODUCTS

ABC of People in the Bible
Colours in the Bible
Breakthroughs
Open Doors
The Seven Spirits of God
Numbers in the Bible
Aglee the Eagle
An Eagle's Life
Chelsea Learns Numbers in Hebrew
ABC's of Faith
Feast of Purim
A Royal Life

Devotionals
31 Day Devotional

Inspirational/Other
Chelsea's Psalms and Poems
Your Daily Meal: Chelsea's Photo Album
Chelsea's Psalms and Poems2
Travel West Caribbean

Puzzle Books
Biblical Puzzle Book Vol 1-5
Bible Puzzles for Young Children Book 1-3
Biblical Puzzle for Children Books 1-5

Teaching Series
How to Hear God's Voice Teaching Guide & Audio Book
Relationship with God, Jesus, Holy Spirit Guide
Knowing God, Jesus, Holy Spirit Guide & Audio Book
Flowing in the Prophetic

Teaching (Non-Sale on my website)
Purim
Passover
Resurrection

BOOK REVIEWS

More books on Amazon, Kobo, and Barnes and Noble, Smashwords, and IngramSpark.
https://chelseak532002550.wordpress.com/

More books on Amazon, Kobo, and Barnes and Noble, Smashwords, and IngramSpark.
https://www.amazon.com/author/chelseakong

Please leave a review and share with friends to help the author continue to write more books to reach more readers. Thank you so much for your support.

Review!

COACHING PRODUCTS

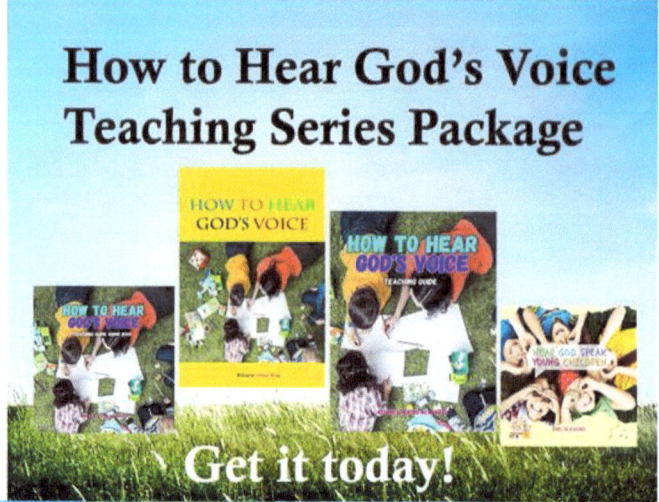

Great books for children. You can get the books individually through Amazon and Barnes and Noble.
https://chelseak532002550.wordpress.com/

COACHING PRODUCTS

Great books for adults.
You can get the books individually through Amazon.
https://chelseak532002550.wordpress.com/

More books coming!

About
CHELSEA KONG

She is a writer, creative arts and digital media artist, skilled administration and payroll professional, and podcaster. Chelsea also served in a variety of roles, from audiovisual, photography, to assisting on the worship team, and ministry team. She also has a passion for families being united.

Chelsea has been a guest on Unity Live Radio, The Lady Tracey Show, and How to Live for Christ and is highly recommended by a Proud Christian blog. She is also a guest blogger. A few of her books have been featured in YourAuthorHub, etc. She graduated from Hotel and Restaurant Management, Digital Media Arts, Office Administration, and is a Payroll Professional. She has experience working with children. Chelsea lives in Toronto, Canada. She mainly writes children's books, stories, bridal writing, poems, lyrics for songs, words of encouragement, blessings, prayers, and jokes. The author of How to Hear the Voice of God, the Bridal Collection, Knowing God, etc. She also has her own Bible Puzzle books and other inspired products. Her podcast channel is called Chelsea K on Anchor, Spotify, and iTunes.

Please check my website to find out more:
https://chelseak532002550.wordpress.com/

www.ingramcontent.com/pod-product-compliance
Lightning Source LLC
Chambersburg PA
CBHW061403090426
42743CB00003B/125